GROWING YOUR CONFIDENCE AND SELF-ESTEEM

Information, Encouragement and Inspirational Short Stories by Teens and Young Adults

Jennifer Leigh Youngs, A.A. · Bettie B. Youngs, Ph.D., Ed.D.

from the SMART TEENS-SMART CHOICES series

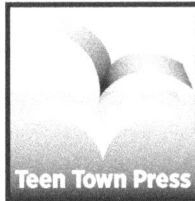

Teen Town Press
www.TeenTownPress.com

an imprint of Bettie Youngs Book Publishers, Inc.

BETTIE YOUNGS BOOKS

Cover Graphic Design: Adrian Pitariu and Beau Kimbrel
Text Design: Beau Kimbrel
Teen Consultant: Kendahl Brooke Youngs

TEEN TOWN PRESS / www.TeenTownPress.com is an Imprint of Bettie Youngs Book Publishing Co., Inc.
www.BettieYoungsBooks.com • info@BettieYoungsBooks.com.

If you are unable to order this book from your local bookseller or online, or Ingram Book Group, you may order directly from the publisher: info@BettieYoungsBooks.com.

PRINT ISBN: 978-1-940784-86-1
DIGITAL ISBN: 978-1-940784-87-8

10 9 8 7 6 5 4 3 2

Library of Congress Cataloging-in-Publication Data Available upon Request.

Summary: Information on enhancing self-confidence, self-esteem, and inspirational short stories by teens and young adults.
1. YAN literature. 2. Teens and Young Adults. 3. Self-Esteem.
4. Confidence. 5. Self-Reliance. 6. Self-worth.
7. Youngs, Bettie Burres. 8. Youngs, Jennifer Leigh.

Also by the Authors for Teens and Young Adults

How Your Brain Decides If You Will Become Addicted—Or Not

Setting and Achieving Goals that Matter TO ME

Managing the Stress, Pressure and the Ups and Downs of Life

The 10 Commandments and the Secret Each One Guards—FOR YOU

How to Be Courageous

Growing Your Confidence and Self-Esteem

Faith at Work in Our Lives

Understanding Feelings of Love

Understanding the Christian Faith

How to be a Good Friend

Having Healthy and Beautiful Hair, Skin and Nails

The Power of Being Kind, Courteous and Thoughtful

How to Have a Great Attitude

Caring for Your Body's Health and Wellness

Daily Inspiration

Inspirational Stories and Encouragement on Friends and the Face in the Mirror

CONTENTS

CHAPTER 1
The All-Important Sense of Self

Self-esteem is self-regard. It's how much you cherish and appreciate being you. It's the "price tag" you place on yourself: what is your worth—are you a valuable commodity, or a "markdown"?

Have you noticed how some people are very comfortable being themselves? Leanna Simons is that way. Her friends say, "Leanna has such a nice presence about her, such a positive sense of self."

Self-esteem is like that. Self-esteem shows up in how you treat yourself. It shows up in what you say and do, and how you treat others.

Self-Esteem is a Self-Picture

What we think of ourselves advertises to others what we think of ourselves—and they will pretty much treat us accordingly. Think of it: When you're deciding what to wear, do you handle a "good shirt" more carefully than an everyday tee-shirt? The way you communicate (your choice of words, your tone and style of relating, how well you listen), as well as how you present yourself (your appearance, your manners), are just a few of the many telltale signs of how much you value, honor and respect yourself.

Psychologists say that self-esteem has a direct effect on all aspects of your health—mental, physical, social and emotional. Healthy self-esteem serves you well. Not so for low self-esteem. Those with low self-esteem are more likely to treat others unfairly, be inconsiderate of the feelings of others, or engage in self-destructive behaviors such as smoking, or using drugs.

Because the way you think of yourself is evident in what you say and do, how you feel about yourself is often obvious to the people around you. But what is most important, is what YOU think of you.

"Just Me, Love Dan"

Because your self-regard is reflected in your behavior, other people can readily see what you think of yourself. Seventeen-year-old Dan said that once when he wrote his girlfriend a letter and signed it "Just me, Love Dan" she gave the letter back to him, telling him she didn't like the way he signed it.

"Why?" he asked. She replied, "I'd like to think that I'm going out with someone who thinks more of himself than 'just me.' When you say, 'just me,' I take it to mean you don't think of yourself as very special, so I must not be all that special either. I don't want to go out with a guy who thinks of himself or me as 'nobody special.'"

Dan realized she was right. "I decided to stop talking (and writing) about myself in a way that made me look as though I am not a person who thinks of himself in a more positive way," said Dan. "I want Katrina to know that I appreciate her and deserve someone so caring and lovely. And, just as I sign my letters to Katerina with 'Love, Dan' to let her know that my feelings for her are positive and loving, the words I say to me should be as positive and loving, too."

INTRINSE WORTH: THE CONFIDENCE YOU HAVE IN YOU

As Katerina explained to Dan, self-worth shows how you feel about yourself. It's the level of your self-confidence in YOU. This self-picture affects how you value and care for your well-being. It shows up in how meticulous you are in your grooming; the friends you choose and how you treat them (and others); the goals you set and achieve, and how self-aware you are.

Brent, 16, had a habit of belittling others. "Another bad hair day, Susan?" he'd snicker to a classmate if her hair wasn't particularly as neat and well-groomed as she usually kept it. "Nothing zinc wouldn't cure," was a favorite phrase of his when a classmate had scored low on a test or quiz or done poorly on a homework assignment. This comment was usually followed by Brent waving his high marks or good score in the air for the other students to see.

Brent made others feel bad as he bragged about himself; it was as if he needed to make others feel "less" in order for him to feel "more." Brent's sense of bravado came at another's expense. But this is not "high" self-esteem. In fact, it's an example of low self-esteem.

If Brent had felt better about himself, then he wouldn't have found it necessary to be so critical of others, nor attempt to make others feel inadequate.

BEING "AUTHENTIC"

With a healthy self-esteem, far from being conceited or self-centered, you have an authentic sense of self. This means you understand that you are human. You have good days. You have bad days. You have ordinary days. You are awesome and capable of greatness. You are vulnerable and will sometimes fail at things.

Allowing for both the ups and downs, taking the good with the bad, gives you a more realistic sense of self, a compassionate sense of self. This is called "being authentic," meaning to be "real." If you can imagine and accept this range of emotions within yourself, then you can imagine and accept this range within others. This is what it means to understand and show consideration to others.

THE BENEFITS OF A HEALTHY SELF-ESTEEM

There are many important benefits of a healthy self-esteem. Here are a few of them.

- The healthier your self-esteem, the more accepting and honoring you are of yourself.

You like yourself. You want YOU as a friend.

- The healthier your self-esteem, the more you take care of yourself. Because you value your health and wellness, you do the things that protect them.

- The more you appreciate yourself, the less likely it is that you will compare yourself with others. Your measuring stick for judging yourself is within.

- The healthier your self-esteem, the better able you will be to find ways to get along well with others. With a healthy self-esteem you form close relationships with people who respect and value you.

- The healthier your self-esteem, the more likely you will treat others with respect and fairness, since self-respect is the basis of respect for others.

- The healthier your self-esteem, the more you will attract others who enjoy their lives and are working to their potential. People with low self-esteem tend to seek low-self-esteem friends, who also think poorly of themselves.

- The healthier your self-esteem, the better able you are to cope with the ups and downs of life. Teens with a healthy self-esteem have a realistic view of their strengths and weaknesses and maintain a positive attitude when they fail at a task.

- The healthier your self-esteem, the more likely you will be to think about what you want out of life, the more ambitious you will be in going after it and the more likely you will be to achieve it.

- The healthier your self-esteem, the more you will confront obstacles and fears, rather than avoid them. Low-esteem individuals see problems as grounds for quitting and often say to themselves, "I give up."

- The healthier your self-esteem, the more able you are to recognize your own worth and achievements without a constant need for approval from others.

- The healthier your self-esteem, the more responsibility you take for your own actions. When you recognize that you are off course, you are more likely to self-correct, to stop going in a negative direction and begin anew.

- The healthier your self-esteem, the more willing you are to hang in there, even when the going gets tough. Because you persist, your chances for experiencing success are greater. The more success you experience, the less likely it is that you will feel devastated or deflated by periodic setbacks.

• The healthier your self-esteem, the happier you are. And a happy person with a smile is a beautiful person who makes other people want to be around him or her.

As you can see, the picture you have of you is impactful. It affects so much. Take a moment now to write down why you feel self-esteem is important.

CHAPTER 2

You Can Change Your Self-Esteem

You can change your self-esteem, but it's not a yo-yo. You don't just wake up one day with a high self-esteem or a low self-esteem. It's not like having a good hair day and a bad hair day. On some days, it seems like your hair has a mind of its own and it won't do what you want no matter what, but self-esteem isn't like that.

Your self-esteem is the whole picture of how you see yourself. Experts say that this picture is the product of about a year's worth of "pictures." Here's the way it works:

SELF-PICTURE #1:

Let's say that you are an average student in math. For most of this past year, you received Cs. If this is the case, when friends ask you if you are "good at math," chances are you will say, "average." So if you get an A on a test during this year when you see yourself as an average student, you will be very happy (or think it was "just luck"), but the one A is unlikely to change your mind about being an "average" student in math.

SELF-PICTURE #2

Let's say that you have been getting Cs for the first three months of in math, and then, for the next three months you have been earning mostly As. How do you see yourself, as a C student or an A student? If you see yourself as earning As more and more consistently, your view of yourself as a C student is going to change.

That's the way it is with esteem. If the picture you had of yourself in the past was of someone who doesn't speak up for yourself, of having low self-confidence, or as someone in the habit of putting yourself down, but you want to change that, you can. Deciding to be a positive person, and by setting goals to be more friendly and courteous, you gain the respect of others (and yourself as well).

Changing your image with others begins with changing it for YOU.

SELF-ESTEEM FUELS YOUR CONFIDENCE

That self-esteem can change is good, but it can go from good to bad, too. If you have been a good student in math for a while, but then start being late to class, skip assignments and doing poorly in class, then chances are you are going to lose confidence in yourself as being a good student in math class. But if you take responsibility for your actions and behavior and work toward turning things around, then your confidence grows stronger.

> Self-esteem is a consequence of your actions. The more you act in positive and affirming ways, the better (healthier) it is, and the better you respect and honor yourself and others.

HOW TO HAVE A GOOD REPUTATION WITH YOURSELF

Because self-esteem is so important, you need to know how to take care of yours. A healthy self-esteem is a result—a consequence of behaving in positive ways.

Here are the things you can do to have a "good reputation" with yourself:

✓ Believe that you have a right to live a happy and fulfilling life and set healthy behaviors as goals.

✓ Take good care of your body. Don't take risks that could put your safety and your health in jeopardy (such as using drugs and alcohol or riding in a car with someone who does).

✓ Get to know and understand yourself and make friends with the face in the mirror. Treat yourself with respect. Don't put yourself down with sarcasm or hurtful words. Others will take your lead and treat you as you treat yourself. Remember, you are the one setting this standard.

✓ Make choices consistent with values you know to be good and right, those you can be proud to stand up for.

✓ Set worthy goals and strive to achieve them.

✓ Develop a "can-do" attitude, but accept that just as you have strengths, you have weaknesses. Everyone has both.

✓ Take time out regularly to be alone with yourself so that you can listen to yourself and ponder your inner thoughts and feelings. Cultivate activities you can enjoy by yourself, like crafts, reading or an individual sport. The goal is to become your very best friend, to truly enjoy your own company.

✓ Learn effective ways to manage the normal ups and downs of stress and pressure.

✓ Practice your faith. Faith is about the timeless truths and provides leadership to your heart and soul—the core of your being.

✓ Read broadly and expose yourself to great

minds. This allows you to examine your own assumptions, and to grow and become wise. Refuse to narrow and close your mind so that assumptions are never examined.

✓ Reach out to others to talk about how things are going for you, especially family and friends.

✓ Especially when life seems particularly stressful, it's time to be extra good to yourself. Get adequate rest, eat properly and get the exercise your body needs to burn off tension.

✓ Strive to be happy. Healthy self-esteem is about the "price tag" you put on yourself. A healthy self-esteem contributes to your confidence, and to your doing better and being better. It a real factor in your overall happiness.

✓ Ask for help and support when you need a helping hand. Reaching out is a sign of strength.

In Challenging Times, Ask For Help

Learning how to cope effectively with your life can help you be a happy person—and that's the goal. But sometimes the stress and strains are simply too big for you to handle alone. Asking for help when you need it is a sign of strength and a mark of a person with a healthy self-esteem.

Should you be facing struggles that seem

overwhelming, rather than suffer alone or resort to doing things that are self-destructive, confide in others. It's only natural that sometimes you'll mess up. When this happens, admit it, talk about it, apologize for your shortcomings, and then vow to do better. This shows maturity. And you'll feel better about yourself and more confident in getting through other challenging times.

Parents, teachers and other professionals such as school nurses or counselors were once teens (and many are the parents of teens) and know what it feels like to be unsure of yourself, to have fears and anxieties about coping with life in general.

Trust that adults have the best interest of young people at heart and want to help you make the best choices in dealing with the things going on in your life. It can be scary to tell your parents that you feel in over your head on something for fear that they will be upset with you. Even if you think they will be upset, even if you feel you have let your parents down, tell them anyway because once they work through their own fears and feelings, most always they will get to work to help you sort things out. After all, your well-being is their number-one concern, so brave their reaction and know that in the end, your parents want what's best for you and will do all they can to help you.

CHAPTER 3

It's Not Always, "All about You"

When we seek to discover the best in others, we somehow bring out the best in ourselves. —William Arthur Ward

Self-esteem is the picture we hold of ourselves. What we think of ourselves shows up in the things we say and do. We may even misinterpret the words and actions of others because of the view we hold of ourselves. It's important to see ourselves in the most positive light that we can.

Seeing the good in ourselves helps us to do better, to "be" better. We all have days when almost everything about our lives looks bleak. On those days, it's easy to feel bad about ourselves. Looking on the bright side of things can help us transform tough times: "Just because I'm having a difficult time in one subject doesn't mean that I'm not a good student," or, "Even though someone doesn't want to be my friend, doesn't mean I'm not a likable, friendly and worthy person."

Psychologists tell us that we are hurt less by the calamities of life than we are by how we see them. And this is true when applied to how we see ourselves. Not only do we have the choice to paint the events and situations in our lives in the color that we choose, we also have the choice to paint ourselves in the color we choose. In other words, you get a say in how you see yourself and you do this even while valuing the opinions of others.

From becoming a better athlete, to getting better grades; from being a friend, to attracting better friends; from getting along with your parents, to being granted more privileges; from liking the face in the mirror, to being your number one cheerleader, self-esteem plays a big role.

ARE YOU GOOD TO YOU?

Learning how to nurture yourself, being attentive to your own needs and interests, leads to a sense of being "in sync" within your life. This internal sense of confidence and peace provides a feeling of contentment and harmony. But excessive self-absorption creates a profound sense of loss, of alienation and isolation from ourselves. Like the expression goes, "No man is an island."

We need others.

As we grow in self-awareness and understand the importance of feeling at peace with ourselves, we move from concentrating solely on the self and its internal experience of harmony, to an outward sense of harmony with others. Having developed skills for seeing into yourself, and having learned to appreciate what you see, you can now apply these skills of "seeing into me," to "seeing into you." It's an important venture.

As we turn our focus outward, moving from "me" to "you" adds yet another dimension to our inner contentment. It makes us happy. The more harmonious the relationships we have with others, the greater our inner satisfaction—in a word, happiness.

From "Me-ness" to "You-ness"

Family is a most important source of self-esteem. Bob Byers said it best, "Of all my friends, those who have good relationships with their families are happier than those who are constantly on the outs with them. As for me, I always feel happiest when I'm in a 'good place' with my family—and with my friends."

Bob is right. What would life be like if you didn't have good friends? We all rely on harmony with friends as an important source of contentment. Says Stephanie, "For me, a good friend is someone I can count on, someone with whom I can relax and just hang out, have fun and share my innermost thoughts, deep, dark secrets, lofty and noble goals, or my hopes, joys and fears. I know a friend is a good friend when I feel that with her it is okay, a safe space, to share my deepest thoughts and needs, without worry of being judged, criticized or made to feel silly for feeling the way I do. Friends cheer each other on, laugh and cry together, and just plain commiserate and listen to each other. That's why friends are friends."

Friends help you to grow into being who you are and allow you to reveal those parts of yourself that you may be meeting for the first time. What a wonderful gift. From coping with a disappointment to dealing with the everyday ups and downs of life, friends are important in our lives.

Having people who are "there for us" as a source of strength, support and rejuvenation is not only special, but important. It contributes to our confidence that otherslike and accept us.

Positive Relationships Build Confidence

Feeling supported and needed by friends is good for your self-confidence. Take a moment to think about who provides this source of comfort to you. Hold these relationships close to your heart and protect them by staying in touch and showing your support, remembering to offer them comfort in return.

There are many ways you can share good feelings with others.

Helping others feel good about themselves will make you feel better about yourself. Open doors for people young and old, offer to help, say a kind word, pick up a piece of trash even though it wasn't you who discarded it. Volunteer in your community. Be a person who likes people. We live in a world with others. It is our obligation—as much as it is our honor—to help others see their lives in a positive light.

From saving a lizard to building homes for Habitat for Humanity or the Fuller Center for Housing, there are many ways to get involved in the lives of others. Some of these can be as simple as being good to the people we meet in our everyday lives.

- Help someone who is ill, infirm or broken-hearted. Feel how good it is to provide strength when another needs it.

- Assist someone. If you see someone drop something, offer help gathering things. Watch the gratitude on that person's face.

- Diligently care for your pets. Allow yourself to feel the happieness your pet gives to you.

- Compliment others, even those you don't know, on how nice they look, whether it be the smile on their face, or the clothes they are wearing.

In doing these things, you'll find goodwill produces confidence with self, and others. There's nothing more esteem-building than when we all feel in harmony with one another. In the workbook part of this book, you'll get a chance to discover ways to be a good friend to yourself, and others.

CHAPTER 4

Selfhood: Learning to Be Ourselves

Each of us longs to "be ourselves." And yet, we seek the approval of others:

✓ "Do you think I'm okay?"
✓ "Do you accept me as I am?"
✓ "Do you like the way I look?"
✓ "Do you approve of how I act?"
✓ "Do you like me?"
✓ "Will you be my friend?"

We want the answers to each of these questions to be a wholehearted "Yes!" When others like us and accept us, we feel worthy—like we're a terrific person. But even though we may want to feel liked and accepted by others, we may not always get a positive response; some people may not think as much of us as we would like. Sometimes this doesn't bother us, but most of the time, especially if their approval is important to us, it's only natural to feel rejected, hurt or left out.

All of us are vulnerable to the scrutiny of others. Why are we so sensitive to their review of us? We want them to accept and approve of who we are at our inner level, not just for what they see of us at the surface. What we really want is for others to like and accept us for who we are—as we are. But what if they don't like what they see? The fear of being rejected is at the heart of the struggle between hiding and revealing ourselves and can cause us to feel as though even the people closest to us don't really understand us very well.

Many young people believe that in order to win favor and friendship from others, they have to "play into" or portray an image they believe someone else holds of them, rather than "be themselves." It's a coat of paint they aren't all that happy about wearing: the price-tag for being "someone else" comes at a loss of our own identity. Sometimes the loss includes self-respect and self-esteem—our own.

The good news is, while you are willing to do some things to gain acceptance, there's a limit, and then we begin to feel uncomfortable about it. Feeling uneasy about covering up who you are in order to be liked by someone else is a healthy feeling. You are you and that is who you are supposed to be. You shouldn't have to become someone you're not.

The Image You Hold of Yourself is Also Shaped by Others

The image we hold of ourselves is often influenced or colored by others. It's easy to get pulled in a lot of different directions, especially when you're trying to meet the expectations of others, all of whom are important to you. There's a fine line between going along, doing the things others want you to do, and being true to yourself, listening to your own voice and preferences, acting on what you believe, and doing what's important and best for you.

Pleasing My Parents

As Jennifer explains, "A big image I had of myself was as an athlete in high school, more specifically, as a pitcher on my school softball team. Just before I'd wind up to throw a pitch, I'd look up in the bleachers and see my mother's smiling face, confident I'd strike out the batter. I'd hear, 'You can do it, Jen!' Meanwhile I was thinking, 'I just hope this pitch goes somewhere in the direction of the plate and not a half-mile over the batter's head and out of the ballpark entirely!' I wasn't nearly as certain as you were of my pitching skills. Then I'd look over at Dad who had reminded me on more than one occasion, 'Jen, you're better at soccer. That's your best chance for a scholarship. That's where you should be concentrating your time.' All the while, I was wishing I could concentrate on my first love—tennis.

"Once a friend of mine asked me if my favorite sport was softball, soccer or tennis. 'Softball,' I answered. But I thought about it for a minute and knew softball wasn't my favorite sport. My answer was based on the gratification I felt having my parent's excitement at my playing softball. On the way home from the games, whether our team won or lost, my parents always thought I played well, no matter what. In your eyes, I could do no wrong. It was a very good feeling.

"Correcting myself, I said to my friend, 'Actually, I prefer soccer.' But once again, I realized that there were conditions around my playing soccer that made me continue to play it. A couple of times a week, and sometimes on the weekends, Dad spent time with me, teaching me soccer skills. And, he came to practically every soccer game and once, after one of the games, he told me I was 'the most powerful athlete on the team.'

"Many young people can relate. Like pleasing my parents was a big appeal of my playing softball and soccer, I'm betting a few kids sit at the piano when they're first learning to play, do not say, 'I'm practicing for the next half-hour without complaining because I see myself as a great pianist, the next Beethoven.' More likely they're saying, 'I'm practicing because in thirty minutes, I'll get a hug, a bowl of ice cream, time with my friends, phone privileges, and avoid being in trouble with my mom (or dad) for not practicing!'

"And by the way, parents aren't the only conflicting voices. There are the expectations of friends, teachers and coaches. I personally remember one coach who promised that if we had a good game, he'd take the team out for pizza. Talk about motivation for teacher-pleasing!"

"Painting" Ourselves for the Sake of Others

Being pulled in so many directions by so many people, all of whom you genuinely want to please, can make you seem as though you need a "paintbrush" to color yourself differently for others!"

That parents, teachers and even your friends see you differently than you see yourself is one of the reasons so many young people relate to the poem, "The Paintbrush":

THE PAINTBRUSH

I keep my paintbrush with me, wherever I may go,
In case I need to cover up, so the real me doesn't show.

I'm so afraid to show you me; afraid of what you'll do,
I'm afraid you'll laugh or say mean things; afraid I might lose you.

I'd like to remove all the layers, to show you the real, true me,
But I want you to try to understand; I need you to like what you see.

So if you'll be patient and close your eyes, I'll remove the coats real slow,
Please understand how much it hurts, to let the

real me show.

*Now that my coats are all stripped off, I feel
naked, bare and cold,
And if you still find me pleasing, you are my
friend, pure as gold.*

*I need to save my paintbrush though, and hold it
in my hand,
I need to keep it handy in case someone doesn't
understand.*

*So please protect me, my dear friend, and thanks
for loving me true,
And please let me keep my paintbrush with me,
until I love me, too.*

—**By Lee Ezell**

CHAPTER 5

Inspirational Short Stories by Teens and Young Adults

You'll get a chance to read stories from young people who share their views about ways they used this imaginary paint brush. Some wanted a paintbrush to cover up, such as 16-year-old Shaun Martin, who confessed he needed one "until the real me . . . will stay around long enough for me to get used to."

Being a young person means constantly growing and changing in many ways. Sometimes many layers of "paint" were needed for more than camouflage—they were needed as protection. This was true for 14-year-old Mia Templett who tells us why each day she paints a smile on her face, and for 13-year-old Alana Ballen, diagnosed with bipolar disorder. And many teens, like 16-year-old Rebecca Holbrook, thought that perhaps adults, too, cover up their real selves, as she feels her mother does because her mom's "life didn't really turn out the way she had hoped."

Other young people wanted to lay their "paintbrush" down, to stop being someone else's shade of friend, as did 15-year-old Marie Benton.

So enthralled that she'd been chosen to do a school project with the all-popular Heather Winslow, Marie found herself shamelessly parading up and down the library mimicking Heather, even though she knew her actions were suspect! It's nice to see that Marie is developing the courage to act in ways that feel right to her.

As Chelsey tells us, "You have to decide how willing you are to sacrifice your true self in order to have others like you." Still, others, like 16-year-old Chad Dalton, said, "My true color comes out when I'm with real friends," and tells us what "color" it takes to be considered his friend. And Eric Chadwick, 17, discovered that when it came to the girl he wanted to date, it was he, and not the girl, who had done the painting!

And, many young people agree that while on occasion they may wear a "coat of paint," beneath its surface is a self you deeply love and honor. And would like the rest of us to love and honor, too.

Will the Real Me Please Stand Up!

Lately I've started to wonder what it means when people say, "Just be yourself!" It's a dumb thing to say to me right now because most of the time I'm not sure who I am! How can I be? I'm constantly changing. I mean, I look and sound totally different than I did just three months ago. Then I had a decent complexion; now it's oily and zit-ridden. Three months ago, my voice sounded like a normal human being's; now it fluctuates between squeaky one day and deep the next, like I'm echoing into a big drum or something. And some of my body parts look like they don't belong with the other parts. I started working out last year, so I was really buffed. But I've grown five inches in the last six months, so I'm gangly and look completely out of proportion. I'm happy about getting taller, except that now my muscles don't look as big and my head looks as if it's sitting on a tall skinny post.

I used to have no problem getting girls to come up and talk with me. Now I've lost confidence that they find me attractive. I worry that if by chance a girl should get interested, it'll only be a matter of time before she'll be turned off by my skin breaking out so much or laugh when my voice does its squeak-and-croak act.

It's not just my body that has changed—everything has. I've always thought of myself as a regular guy; but now, from one day to the next, my emotions are all over the place. One day I feel up, the next down. Some days I think, "Hey, I'm really quite smart," and others, "I'm as dumb as a rock!" One week I'm sure what I want to do with my life, the next, I'm totally unsure.

I'm a wreck! Really, I just want the real me to please stand up and stay around long enough for me to get used to him.

Oh yeah, I need a paintbrush for sure!

—Shaun Martin, 16

Quiet and Shy—Not!

I know there are times when my parents and teachers, even some of my friends, see me differently than I really am. They think I'm quiet and shy, really smart but not very cool. What they don't know is that's who I am when I am with them, but it's not who I really am. The real me comes out when I'm around guys who are more like me—like Tom Henderson and Graham Barry. Tom and Graham bring out the best in me, the real me.

I met Tom and Graham at a Young Scientist contest last year. Tom is from Orem, Utah, and Graham is from Ontario, California. The three of us were among the five finalists in a national competition for Promising New Scientists. As soon as the three of us met, we really hit it off. As we talked about the conference, we discovered that all three of us were interested in laser space debris mitigation, which is the study of the prevention of space garbage damaging satellites and the new space station. It was great to meet other people my age who knew what I was talking about. When I talk about "space garbage," most of the kids at my school just say, "Oh, you mean like asteroid-type things? I played a video game about that once."

Luckily, we met each other on the first day of the conference, so we were able to spend a lot of time together for the entire three days. We ate all our meals together, went to each other's event showings, and went out and saw a little of the city together. Then when we'd get back, even though it was late, we'd talk until 2:00 or 3:00 A.M. It was great! We talked about everything from the best schools to go to, what degrees to get, the kind of jobs we want, and even the names of the best people in each field. We want to study with the pioneers. Both Tom and I want to study with Dr. Claude Phipps from Santa Fe, New Mexico. He's the inventor of ORION, a space debris mitigation company that developed a laser that knocks down space garbage before it does any damage to expensive space vehicles. Some of the space garbage travels at over one thousand miles per second! Although you can't track something as small as a grain of sand, it can still do some real damage. Graham wants to study under Jim Cronin, the physics Nobel Laureate from the University of Chicago.

Even though the three of us don't get a chance to see each other very often, we're still the best of friends. We're always sending articles and newspaper clippings to each other, and sometimes we'll send a copy of a class paper we think the other would find interesting. And we call each other a couple of times a month. That may not sound like a lot of time together, but even so, Tom and Graham are better friends of mine than any of the kids I see every day at school. And they know me better than any of the kids at school know me. The three of us just really understand each other and where we're coming from.

I have more fun with them than anyone else. When I get a phone call or email from either Tom or Graham, it's the best feeling—a real high. I always feel happy and in a good mood, even when I'm working through a problem, when I talk with Tom and Graham. It's like this other person in me wakes up. With them, I'm my "real shade."

—**Chad Dalton, 16**

The Most Beautiful Girl...

We don't always see others the way they are, but rather, as we want them to be. I thought Christina Thomas was the most beautiful girl I had ever seen. It took me a long time to get up the courage to ask her out. Finally, I did. When she accepted, I thought I was the luckiest guy in the world. The feeling was short-lived.

The first couple of times I went out with Christina, I was so nervous (and happy to be with her) that I pretty much just agreed with whatever she said. But as I began to relax around her, I saw a person who was very different from what I had imagined.

I was surprised to discover Christina wasn't very respectful of other people. She was always saying mean things about them, always putting them down. And she was rude to people for no reason.

I only went out with Christina for five weeks.

Now I see the real Christina. I know what Christina Thomas is really like, and I don't think she is nearly as pretty as I thought at first.

I think it's possible to wear two coats of paint, one on the outside and one on the inside. The coat of paint Christina has on the outside is awesome, the one on the inside isn't as impressive.

Seeing her beauty, I thought she must "be" beautiful, but I've learned that people aren't always what they appear to be. But I doubt that Christina

Thomas was ever any different with me than she was with others.

I think that maybe it wasn't Christina who had the paint brush; I was the one who had painted Christina in a "color" she was not.

—Eric Chadwick, 17

The Dragon in My Drawer!

Sometimes when I'm a bit uptight from doing everything just right,

I have a room, my own retreat where I can kick my shoes off of my feet. My desk is cluttered and piled high, even the curtains are awry.

When I look at this untidy mess, "Yes!" I shout. I like it, I do confess. There are things tossed on the floor, a dragon's in my dresser drawer. He guards the clothes not folded right and warns, "Hands off or I shall bite!" Then, before I leave my room, I comb my hair and straighten out the things I wear.

But I'll tell you what—that prim and proper image others see is not the authentic me!

—Elmer Adrian, 90

My Bipolar Disorder

So many things about being a teenager are tough. One of them is making sense of being told "be yourself," when the other part of that message— even though it's silent—is "as long as you're beautiful, cheerful and thin." Everyone wants you to be perfect in every way. I know a lot of kids who "cover up" because it's so impossible to be like we're supposed to be.

I've had a lot of trouble being perfect, especially with the "thin" part. Even though the bathroom scale said I wasn't over-weight, the pounds just didn't seem to sit in the right places. When I looked in the mirror, I was anything but beautiful or perfect. The more I tried to change my body, the less cheerful I felt. I said to my mom, "I'm so fat while all the girls at school are so skinny!"

"You're not at all fat," she said. "Besides, you don't have to be the same as all the girls at school. Just like every flower is beautiful in its own way, being an individual bloom is wonderful for people, too." But I knew better. It would be just great to live in a world where you were liked and considered pretty because being an individual bloom was okay. Instead, you have to be a perfect flower or you aren't going to be selected as good enough for a corsage— to fit in with everyone else.

I've had a lot of trouble with trying to be a

perfect flower. So, I'd cover up with my trusty "paintbrush" so nobody could tell how depressed I was. It can hurt to show people how you really are when you're sure they won't like what they see. My friends, and even some of my classmates, said I was the class clown, always up and on and funny. At the time, it seemed like a good way to prove I was cheerful. But it's a lot of work to always be up and on, funny and witty. I got so tired of it, and then I reached a point where I didn't want to pretend that I was cheerful if I wasn't.

The other kids don't think I am so funny and witty when I am feeling down. They just leave me alone, or tease me, "Oh, the clown forgot her nose today?" Nobody wants to hear that you're having a bad day or that you just "feel down." It's funny how that works, but it's true.

I got so depressed. Depression is a terrible thing because there is no end in sight. I felt like I was in a deep, black hole and couldn't get out. Trying to be perfect while knowing I wasn't only made it worse. I tried almost everything. When nothing worked, I attempted suicide. Now I've been diagnosed with bipolar disorder, so I'm on three kinds of medications: Depakote, Paxil and Ziprexia. Before I was on these medications, I thought the problem was me and that I just wasn't as tough as my friends are. I worried that there was something wrong with me mentally, like maybe I was crazy or something. It's a huge relief to find out that what's wrong with me is called bipolar disorder. It's a medical condition, one that can be straightened out. Before I was diagnosed, my parents told me I did stupid things. My friends saw me as the class clown, who had become a drag. But now that I'm getting medical help, I no longer feel like I have two lives. And I feel less frightened of my feelings. Other people feel confused and overwhelmed sometimes, too. I'm not the only one.

Now that I know what's causing me to feel this way, I can give up painting myself to be someone I am not. I am a girl who needs medication to help my body do what it's supposed to do, to feel like it's supposed to feel. These days I'm worrying less about being perfect enough to fit into a bouquet. I'm just working on being an individual bloom. I like to think of myself as a flower. Forget the class clown act.

—Alana Ballen, 13

Heather's Clone

At times, I cover up the "real me" by acting in ways I think the other person wants or expects me to, rather than acting on who I really am. I did it just yesterday.

I woke up yesterday feeling sort of "blah" but not sick enough to stay home. I would have preferred to stay in bed, but I went to school anyway since I didn't want to fall behind in my homework and have extra over the weekend. I got up late, showered, got dressed in a hurry, ran my fingers through my hair and rushed out the door. I didn't look my best.

Luckily, my first-period teacher didn't have anything ambitious in mind for us. Our class mostly worked on individual assignments at our own desks. I was not so lucky in my second period class. The teacher, Mrs. Whetherill, took our class to the library and assigned us to work in pairs on a research project. I was paired with Heather Winslow!

Heather is one of the most popular girls at school. Some people might call her selective; others might call her uppity. And preppy. Since I'm just one of the average kids at school, Heather smiles when she sees me, but that's about it. It's not like I'm someone she'd consider hanging around with.

Like everyone else, I'd do almost anything to be her friend (or even to be seen with her). And that's pretty much what I did yesterday!

Heather is a perky sort of person, so even though

I wasn't feeling all that well, I put on my I've-got-a-great-personality-and-attitude act. I tried to perk up and be Heather's clone—so she wouldn't mind getting stuck with me for the project. But my transformation didn't end there! The teacher allowed us to walk around the library to get the different reference books we needed for our assigned projects. The two books Heather and I needed were easy to find. But even though we had all the reference books we needed for the project, that didn't stop Heather from pretending we needed others. Heather walked back and forth across the entire length of the library several times— to be seen, of course. I was so happy to be seen with Heather Winslow that I followed her on these aimless jaunts, no doubt looking conspicuous since Heather is more experienced in this sort of thing than I am. I never was quite sure when to appear busy looking for books, or, once I'd attracted attention to myself, when to smile at everyone since it was obvious I had distracted them into noticing me. Heather, of course, had it figured out: She did both.

But I didn't just stop at being Heather's shadow, either! I also tried to sound like her!

Heather giggles all the time. It's a sort of a high-pitched, peculiar sound, one she uses more for getting attention than anything else. As she walked around searching for bogus reference books, Heather giggled loudly enough to get the attention of other students as she walked by them. So did I! I mimicked Heather's giggle even though I'm not someone who normally giggles at every little thing. I'm sure that I sounded totally ridiculous since they'd never heard these strange, quirky little sounds coming from my mouth before. I hadn't either!

At the time, it was fun. Since I was with Heather, everyone looked at us. The problem was, because I didn't feel all that great in the morning, I hadn't bothered to put on anything nicer than jeans, an old sweatshirt and my ratty pair of tennis shoes. My hair looked awful; it was having a bad day, too. Nevertheless, here I was giggling and parading around, drawing attention to myself. I'm sure I looked as ridiculous as I sounded. Being seen with Heather and getting as much attention as she was (or at least more than I was used to) felt good—yesterday, that is. Today I'd describe my feelings about my behavior in the library more as embarrassed than anything else. I know my classmates knew I was showing off, and even worse, I know I was. It's just that sometimes. even when you know you're acting like a dweeb, it's hard not to get caught up in someone else's behavior. Especially when you're with someone like Heather, who has a way of making you feel like you're obligated to go along with whatever she's doing or saying. It's like the chameleon going along with the colors in its surroundings.

Sometimes I feel like a chameleon, changing my colors when I'm around different kinds of people. When I'm not feeling super secure with myself, I act more or less intelligent, athletic or pretty than

I really am. To try to blend in with whoever I'm with, I cover up the "real me" by acting in ways I think the other person wants me to. That's what happened when I got paired up with Heather.

Sometimes you have to do what your friends expect of you because if you don't, you won't have any friends. I know I followed Heather around and tried to be her clone in order to be liked by her. But you know what, it didn't work. The next day Heather acted like she didn't know me! All that work for nothing!

At least I'm aware of what I did—not that it's much of a con- solation. I do want to be true to myself and not have to paint myself over to be someone else's "color." What I'd really like is for Heather to think I'm so cool she'll follow me around and want to be my clone! Now that's a color I'd like to see.

—Marie Benton, 15

The Mask She Wears

Reading "The Paintbrush" made me feel sad for my mother. She works very hard at two jobs and is usually so tired. She has zero social life. Still, she tries to sound upbeat and positive way more than she really feels. I think her life didn't really turn out the way she wanted, and that she hides a lot of disappointments. I know she doesn't like either one of her jobs. And she doesn't like the house we live in. It needs painting and new carpet and a lot of repairs, things we can't afford to do right now. Mom says we should get a newer, smaller place, but a newer, smaller house can't really fix things because the real problem is that Mom doesn't want to live in this town any longer. She and my father divorced last year, and my mother would like to move back near her parents. But I really like the school I go to and I like my friends. When my mother was my age, her father's company transferred him to a different city. She had to leave her friends behind and complete high school in a whole new area. Mom said it was a terrible experience for her. She told me that she doesn't want me to have to go through the same thing. We're going to stay here until I finish high school. I like that idea, but I know it's tough on my mother, one more compromise she's making. Even though Mom acts like it's okay with her, I know it isn't. It must not be much fun to be her.

I appreciate all the things my mother does for

me. I know she works hard at trying to make the best of our situation. I'm trying to do my part, too. I'm trying to complain less about the things I want but know we can't really afford, such as a phone of my own. And I'm trying to be a little more understanding and patient with my mom when she's stressed out.

I guess that sometimes adults have to be someone other than who they'd prefer to be. Sometimes adults paint on a mask, too.

—Rebecca Holbrook, 16

Love, Me

I once wrote my girlfriend a letter and signed it "Just me." It surprised me when she told me she didn't like the way I signed it. "I'd rather go out with someone who thought more of himself than 'just me,'" she commented. "I deserve more than a 'just me' boyfriend."

What she said made me realize that when I wrote "just me," I was really saying "I'm no one special." But that's not how she feels about me, and it's not how I feel about myself, either. When I thought about it, I realized that I underestimated the importance of talking (and writing) about myself in a positive way.

I've decided to give myself a whole new "paint job." I've decided to stop (unconsciously) putting myself down. Before, I'd say things like, "School isn't for me, I'm a horrible student." Even saying or thinking those words made me feel like I was a horrible student and so I'd dislike school even more—which was crazy because it wasn't even true. I'm not a bad student. And I don't hate school. I'm a bright guy, and I like most of my classes.

Now I say things in a better way, a way that doesn't make me get down on myself. Now when I talk about school, I say something like, "I like school even though I'm having a tough time with algebra. When I learn the concepts of algebra that I don't understand right now, I'll get better grades.

I'm going to keep working on it."

By being more positive and not putting myself down, I actually help myself do better. I like it when other people encourage me. It only makes sense that I encourage me, too.

I've learned that what people call positive thinking and positive self-talk is like giving yourself a paint job. Why be a "just me" when I can be a "great guy"? Why be a lousy student, when I can be a student who just has a little trouble with algebra?

I'm glad that my girlfriend made the comment she did because it helped me understand a simple equation: Just as I sign the letters I write to her, "Love, Dan," I can sign thoughts to myself that way, too. When I write "Love, Dan" to her, it's intended to let her know that my feelings for her are positive and loving, so why not make my own thoughts and words to myself as positive and loving as possible, too?

I think the words we use are like a coat of paint. So, be sure you choose the "right" color!

—Dan Belana, 17

I Wouldn't Go Out with Belinda Even If . . .

Brian had been out of school for three days with the flu. On the morning of his return, he noticed a group of friends clustered around talking about Belinda, the "new girl" at school. All of his friends said how cute and fun she was, and how much they were looking forward to sitting with her at the next day's sports assembly. Even though Brian had no idea who Belinda was, he began his usual habit of being critical of others. "I don't think she's all that cute," he remarked. "She's got skinny legs, and my little sister's got bigger boobs than she does. And she ought to get a new hairstyle!"

Though his friends looked on in disbelief, neither their looks of surprise nor expressions of disgust could deter Brian from making even more disparaging remarks about Belinda—whom he knew nothing about. When Brian announced, "I wouldn't go out on a date with Belinda even if she paid me," one girl in the group, Peggy (a girl Brian secretly liked and hoped to ask out), quipped, "Brian, you are really a geek! And don't worry, no one I know—including Belinda—would go out with you, even if you paid her!" Having said that, she turned and walked away.

Belinda, the one Brian thought needed a bigger bosom, shapelier legs and a more modern hairstyle, the one Brian was too good to date (even if she paid him), was the new school mascot. . . a goat!

—**Brian Tracey**

Ferrari, Anyone?

"If think you can or if you think you can't, you're right either way." —Henry Ford

A young boy came home crying from school one day. His grandfather was visiting and greeted him.

"Why are you crying?" his grandfather asked.

"Because Paul called me a sissy! Do you think I'm a sissy, Grandpa?"

"Oh no," said his grandfather. "I think you're a Ferrari."

"A car?" said the boy, trying to make sense of what his grandfather had said.

"Well, if you believe that just because Paul called you a sissy that you really are one, you might as well believe you're a car, and a terrific one at that," explained the grandfather, asking, "Why be a sissy when you can be a Ferrari?"

"Oh! That's cool, Grandpa!" the boy exclaimed, now realizing that he got to have a say in how he felt about himself.

"Yes, it is," replied his grandfather. "The opinion you have of yourself should not only count as much as anyone's—but even more."

—Anonymous

A Ferrari Without an Engine

Last semester, after we had turned in our final class project in our biology class, the teacher told us to assign ourselves a grade based on how well we felt we had done on the project. My buddy, Reese, gave himself an A. He really did do a great job on the project, and probably it was an A project.

I knew my project was even better than his. After completing a unit on mollusks, our class was supposed to do a report of our choosing related to the subject. Reese did his report on the New Zealand Paua, a mollusk with a blue-green iridescent colored shell that's often used in costume jewelry, like in the ring his little sister had. He wrote up his report, and then when he presented it to the class, he showed them his eight-year-old sister's ring.

I decided to do my report on the differences between a natural and cultured pearl. The more I got into reading and researching the pearl, the more interested I became. I really put my heart into the project. I found out that the formation of a pearl is actually the result of an irritant, such as a grain of sand, that has gotten into the shell of the oyster. In order to protect itself from whatever is invading it, whether it's a piece of sand or something that feeds on this sort of mollusk, the oyster secretes a white liquid substance to protect itself. It will encrust anything within its reach. Sometimes when a natural pearl is cut in half, a grain of sand or some small creature is found inside of it.

I was surprised to learn that a pearl's size can vary from between that of a pinhead to that of a pigeon's egg. The Hope Pearl, which is the largest pearl ever found, is nearly two inches long! The Hope Pearl is kept in the South Kensington Museum in London. So, for my report, I wrote the museum and asked for information on the Hope Pearl. They sent me a lot of material, including some really great photographs, which I included in the report. Everyone, especially the teacher, was impressed. This made me feel pretty good because I really put a lot of time and work into my project—and it showed. It was a great report.

I knew that the project I handed in was A quality. Reese's report was good, but mine was much more complex than his. Even so I gave myself a B. And you know what, the teacher gave my friend Reese an A and gave me a B! I think that says a lot about the value we place on ourselves. There was no reason for me to devalue the amount of work and time I had put in on this project to make sure it was excellent. I'm not saying that Reese overvalued his paper, but if his was worth an A, for sure mine was worth one, too! But I didn't stand up for myself and the quality of my work on the project.

It was a good lesson for me. I'm being more honest in presenting my own worth. It's obvious that my buddy Reese considers himself a Ferrari.

And while I would never want to give myself an A when I don't deserve it, I don't want to give myself a B when I deserve an A, either. I know my report was a Ferrari of a report! But it didn't get the A it deserved because its engine stalled—that engine being the confidence I had in myself. If I had considered myself the Ferrari that I am, rather than a Ferrari without an engine, I would have given myself the grade I deserved.

—**Paul Drexler, 17**

Sergio

My sister is dating a really great guy. His name is Sergio, and he's a fireman.

Sergio is definitely a Ferrari.

My sister and Sergio are pretty serious, and I think she'll probably end up marrying him. This really bugs my father, who tells my sister that she can do better than a fireman.

I think my father is being unfair, first of all because it is my sister who has to live with Sergio, not my father. Second, Sergio is one of the nicest people I know. He's polite and considerate to everyone, especially my sister. He takes her to nice restaurants, to concerts and to almost every special event in the community. I think being a fireman is an honorable profession, even though my father says it's not much of a "lifestyle." And I can understand Sergio's wanting to be a fireman. When he was a small boy, his family's home caught on fire late one night. The family was already asleep. Luckily, the fire department arrived within minutes. The house was quickly engulfed with flames. Though Sergio's mother tried to rescue her two small children from their bedroom, she was overcome by smoke inhalation.

Firemen then rescued each member of the family.

Sergio remembers being carried out of the house by a particular fireman, one who kept in touch with Sergio's family over the years. To Sergio, the men who rescued his family and carried him from the terrible fire are heroes. That fireman is the reason they are all alive. Sergio really admires firefighters. And why not? They literally saved his brother and mother's lives. His, too. How can you say that someone who uses his life in such a purposeful way is not as good or worthy as an executive like my father, who makes a lot of money in his job, but doesn't particularly like the people he works with (he's always complaining about them)? Sergio's work, on the other hand, makes him feel important and needed by others. He loves what he's doing and is happy with his life overall. And he constantly works to improve himself. Though he's already graduated from college, he's taking more courses, especially classes about saving lives.

My father said it must be boring being a fireman because of all the "down time on your hands." I don't see it that way at all. Firemen do a lot more than wait around for a fire to happen. From the things that Sergio and my sister tell me about his work, I think it must be interesting. He meets a lot of people and he gets to travel—even out of state. Just last month when a huge forest fire broke out, Sergio was called in to help. When it was all over, Sergio was credited with saving the lives of nearly three hundred wild mustangs and other wildlife!

Regardless of what my father thinks of my sister's boyfriend, I think when Sergio looks at himself in the mirror, he genuinely likes and respects who he sees. I know I really admire him. And I think my sister would be wise to marry someone who is proud and pleased with who he is. Sergio is the kind of guy I'd like to have for a friend—and as a brother-in-law. I'm very happy my sister is with him.

When a person genuinely is comfortable with who he is, it shows. I think Sergio is the kind of person we should all strive to be like.

—Jennifer Jones, 16

Every Time a Cute Girl Walked By ...

I broke up with my girlfriend, Allison, because every time a cute girl walked by, Allison started ragging on her, saying how dumb she was, or criticizing the way the girl looked or what she was wearing. At first it didn't bother me because I told myself I was with a girl who was "cool"—and better than the other girls. But then I realized that what Allison was saying wasn't always true. Some of the girls she put down as dumb were not at all dumb, and they looked just fine to me.

At first, I thought Allison was just jealous of the other girls. But then I asked myself, "Why should Allison be jealous if she believes she's prettier, smarter and dresses nicer than they do?" I came to the conclusion that Allison's habit of putting others down didn't really have anything to do with the other girls. Allison just didn't feel good about herself.

I think Allison thought that if she found something wrong with other people, it made her look better. She made others seem "less" so she could be "more." I really "got it" about Allison at our last Talent Day. Sometimes you don't know how talented your friends are, but at Talent Day students get to share their talents with everyone in the school. Some of the kids sing or play musical instruments, other kids get together and perform a skit. They really get into it, making costumes and props. Talent Day is supposed to be fun, and I think it is. It's a day to display another dimension of yourself. It's great!

At our school's last Talent Day, everyone was laughing, cheering and clapping for a friend who was on stage. Everyone was having a great time—in the audience and on the stage—all except Allison, who for some reason felt it was her place to act as the event's critic. As though she expected a Broadway performance, Allison judged and criticized each person. As usual, she was especially critical of the girls, most especially the popular or cute ones.

There I was enjoying myself and my friends, having a good time, while my girlfriend—sitting right beside me—seemed grouchy about the whole thing. I wasn't sure what to do. You're supposed to feel loyal to your girlfriend, right? I mean, I'm supposed to like her personality and the things she says and does.

On that particular Talent Day, I realized that I disliked more things about her than I liked. Even though Allison is pretty and smart, it didn't make up for her jealousy and put-downs of others. I began to feel bad about myself for being with Allison. I broke up with Allison that day.

Since then, Allison has had two different boyfriends. (She's not with anyone right now.) Maybe they've discovered what I did. It's not really all that much fun to be with someone who continually puts everyone down.

I think that when you bad-mouth other people,

it's a sign that you don't feel all that secure about yourself. I've decided that no matter how cool you are (or think you are), when you tear others down, it takes away from your image of being "cool"—from being a Ferrari.

For people who put others down, think of this: In the end, you're going to find yourself alone, like Allison.

—Shawn Hamilton, 19

Because I'm So Smart

Kids always tell me that I get good grades because I'm naturally smart. I don't see it that way at all. I mean, if I am so smart then I wouldn't have to work so hard at getting good grades— which I do.

Good grades don't come easy for me. If I were smarter, getting good grades would be so much easier.

My dad says I shouldn't be so tough on myself. He says that if I encouraged myself instead of putting myself down, then getting good grades would be easier for me.

I have a history exam coming up and I want to do well on it. My dad says I should see myself doing well and say positive things to myself like, "I'm going to get a good grade on the exam. I've read the chapters; I've studied; I know the material." I think basically what he's telling me is to see myself as smart so I get smart.

I'll keep you posted if my dad's theory works.

—**Noreen Nicoles, 14**

How Big Is Your Splash?

Now as I look inward,
I find that by comparison, I haven't jumped as high or made as large a splash as others that I know.

I'm told there is no face or mind like mine.
I am one of a kind.

This makes me wonder what another person with the same frame, background and foibles would have done with it.

—Elmer Adrian, 90

My Step-Dad is a Really Great Guy

My father really dislikes my stepfather, Mike, and is always calling him names, saying what a "good-for-nothing" guy he is. Mike knows about his name-calling because sometimes when my father comes to pick me up, he'll say inconsiderate things right in front of my stepdad like, "Is what's-his-name going to pick you up after the game, or am I supposed to bring you home?"

Even though it's rude that my father doesn't call Mike by his name, my stepdad doesn't hold it against my father. "Sure, I'll pick up BeShawn at 3:30," he'll answer. Nor does Mike make a big deal about my father's inconsiderate attitude towards him. He lets the comments go.

I asked my stepfather if the way my father treats him bothers or upsets him. "Oh, not really," he said. "You don't always have to be right, as long you do what's right." I like it that Mike is secure with himself. My father's taunts don't bother Mike because he likes himself. My dad's opinion of my stepdad doesn't change the way Mike feels about himself.

I really admire Mike. I especially like how he's good to my mother. And I really like what a good father he is to me. I appreciate all the things he does for me, like teaching me to throw a fastball and helping me with my homework, without becoming impatient like my father does. Mike even volunteered at my school's carnival this year. No other stepdads were there.

Though I would never tell my real father that I think my stepfather is one of nicest guys I know, he is. I'm happy to have Mike as my stepfather. Sometimes, I even call Mike "Dad" because he acts like a dad to me. In my eyes, my stepfather is a really great guy. I've decided to stay respectful, because I do respect that he is such a great stepdad to me.

—**Shawn Niles, 13**

CHAPTER 6

YOUR PERSONAL WORKBOOK

Our life is like a piece of paper on which every passerby leaves a mark.

—Chinese Proverb

What does this saying mean to you?

_____

_____

Who has left the greatest "mark" on your life—and why do you believe this?

_____

_____

Every artist dips his brush into his own soul, and paints his own nature into his picture—as he does in living his life.
—Henry Ward Beecher

What does this quote mean to you?

_____

_____

What is your paintbrush—how do you "cover up" when you need to?

_____

_____

_____

_____

_____

An Identity of My Own

Do you ever "play into" or portray an image you believe someone else holds of you even though it's "not you"? For example, do you wear your hair in a certain style (or color) or dress or behave in a certain way because you think someone else will like you better if you do?

_____

_____

Describe a time when you "covered up" who you are in order to gain someone's acceptance or approval. What did you do? What were you covering up? What "image" were you trying to present? Whose acceptance or approval were you trying to win?

_____

_____

Did it work—was that person impressed? Did he or she like you better as a result of the image you presented? Did you "fool" that person into thinking you were who you represented? How do you know? How did you feel about the whole thing? If you fooled someone, how did this make you feel about that person?

_____

_____

_____

Why did you feel you had to act in a way other than your authentic self?

_____

_____

_____

What Do You Think About Me?
Do You Accept Me as I Am?

It's only natural to want to be liked and accepted by others. Though we may not always ask aloud, we are always wondering:

"Do you think I'm okay?"

"Do you like the way I look?"

"Do you approve of how I act?"

"Do you like me?"

"Do you accept me as I am?"

"Do you like the way I dress?"

"Will you stick by me in good times and

bad?"
"Will you be my friend—always?"

What else would you add to this list?

❤ _____

❤ _____

❤ _____

❤ _____

❤ _____

❤ _____

❤ _____

❤ _____

❤ _____

❤ _____

❤ _____

❤ _____

We want the answer to each of these questions to be an enthusiastic "Yes!" When others like us and accept us, we feel valued—like we're a terrific person. And that's a good feeling.

Who, more than anyone else, makes you feel

like a "terrific" person?

_____

What does that person do to make you feel so good about yourself, so special? For example: Does he or she support you in being your best? Is he or she patient with you? Does he or she give you the benefit of the doubt? Does he or she trust you? Is he or she a good listener, one who always pays close attention to what you say? Does he or she respect your opinion even if it is different than his or her own? Can you count on this person to be on your side when your values are put to the test—such as being pressured to smoke, drink, do drugs? Is this person kind to you, sensitive to your feelings and gentle with your heart?

_____

_____

_____

Knowing others is intelligence;
knowing yourself is true wisdom.
—Tao Te Ching

List six things that person says or does that make you feel like a terrific person.

❤ _____

❤ _____

❤ _____

❤ _____

❤ _____

❤ _____

How does this "positive review" contribute to the image you hold of yourself?

_____

_____

Who counts on you to see him or her as being special? Why does this person value you in this way?

_____

_____

_____

What three things do you do that create a positive picture for that person?

1. _____

   _____

2. _____

   _____

3. _____

   _____

Who I Am . . . Accept Me as I Am . . .

Even though we may want to feel accepted by others, it doesn't always work out that way. Sometimes this doesn't bother us, but most of the time, especially if their approval is important to us, we feel rejected, hurt or left out. It's only natural to feel this way.

Write about a time when you really wanted a certain person to think well of you and it just didn't happen. Who was the person? How long had you been hoping to gain this person's friendship before you realized there wasn't much of a chance? Why didn't he or she "like" you? How do you know if this was really the case? How did not gaining this person's friendship or acceptance make you feel about yourself? How did it make you feel about the other person?

_____

_____

_____

_____

_____

Do you think it's important to always work toward getting others to like us? How important is it to you?

_____

_____

_____

_____

When someone doesn't like you as much as you would like them to, how does it change the way you feel about yourself?

_____

_____

What do you do when someone doesn't like you as much as you would like? For example, do you write that person a letter telling him or her about your feelings? Or do you go on about your business, reminding yourself that you have other friends and focusing on being a good friend to them—and to yourself? Do you withdraw, feel sad or cry?

_____

_____

_____

How long does it take you to get over feeling rejected?

_____

_____

If a friend asked you for advice on what he or she should do if having a difficult time gaining the friendship or acceptance of someone, what would you tell your friend?

_____

_____

_____

_____

What do you try to cover up about yourself? What are you most afraid that others will not like about you? Why do you think they won't like that part of you?

_____

_____

_____

Who Am I? . . . I Am . . .

Sometimes I am meeting a part of myself for the first time.

—Jennifer Leigh Youngs

What do you think Jennifer's quote means?

_____

_____

_____

Everyone is always saying, "Be yourself," but who is your "true self" anyway? Are you shy or outspoken? Fun-loving or laid back? Are you sporty, artsy, spiritual, intellectual? Write down words or phrases that best describe you.

I am:

_____

_____

_____

Who Do You Think I Am?

Do your friends see you as you see yourself? Ask a good friend to describe you.

My name is _____ and I would describe

_____ as a person who is _____

_____

_____

Now ask your mom to describe you.

I am _____ 's mother, and I would describe

_____ as a person who is: _____

_____

_____

Now ask your dad to describe you.

I am _____ 's dad, and I would describe

_____ as a person who is: _____

_____

_____

Who understands you—the real you—better than anyone else? How do you know this? Why is it this person is able to understand you? How long have you known this person? Do you think you will be friends all of your lives?

_____

_____

_____

Describe a time you felt sure someone "really knew you," and then something happened that made you realize that person didn't know you as well as you thought. For example, did someone ever mistrust you or doubt your word? What happened? What was the incident that showed you this person didn't know the real you? Who was the person? How did you feel about what happened?

_____

_____

_____

How did the incident change the relationship between the two of you? Did it strain the friendship, or make it stronger? Are you still friends or did you part company? What did the incident teach you?

_____

_____

_____

Write about a time you felt someone close to you understood you even better than you understood yourself. Who was this person? What was the situation or circumstance that brought about this understanding?

_____

_____

_____

Who looks outside dreams; who looks inside wakes.
                    —C. G. Jung

Actions: Getting to Know Me

When someone knows you even better than you know yourself, how does it make you feel about the person? In what ways does it make that person even more special to you?

_____

_____

_____

When someone knows you really well, how can that help you understand or know yourself even better?

_____

_____

_____

What I Wished My Friends Knew About Me

Sometimes we need to help our friends get to know "the real me." What two things do you wish your friends knew about you? Why don't they know? How can you let them know?

The first thing I wished my friends knew:

_____

_____

_____

They don't know because:

_____

_____

_____

I can let them know by:

_____

_____

_____

The other thing I wished friends knew:

_____

_____

_____

They don't know because:

_____

_____

_____

I can let them know by:

_____

_____

_____

One Thing I Wished My Family
Knew About Me

What one thing do you wish all of your family members knew about you? Why don't they know? How can you let them know?

I wish all my family members knew:

_____

_____

_____

They don't know because:

_____

_____

_____

I can let them know by:

_____

_____

_____

When do you plan to do this?

_____

_____

_____

When you're a teenager, you get pulled in a lot of different directions, especially when you're trying to meet the expectations of different people—all of whom are important to you.

—Jennifer Leigh Youngs

Have you ever felt as Jennifer describes?

_____

_____

Expectations

Name the three people whose expectations of you matter the most to you. Next to the person's name, describe what it is he or she expects of you.

EXAMPLE:

Who: My Mom.

Expectation: She expects me to be a good student.

How I feel about meeting this expectation: I want to get good grades, too, and I'm glad she believes that I'm smart enough to get them. Still, the added pressure of knowing how disappointed she'll be if I don't do well really stresses me out.

EXAMPLE:

Who: A friend.

Expectation: A friend expects me to be her friend, even when she does things I don't like, such as expecting me to let her copy my homework.

How I feel about meeting this expectation: I feel uncomfortable when I have to just go along with things I don't feel right about—like with copying my homework, sometimes I don't mind, but sometimes I do.

The Real Me . . . Do You Know Me? The Real Me?

1. Who: _____

   Expectation: _____

   _____

   How I feel about meeting this expectation:

   _____

   _____

2. Who: _____

   Expectation: _____

   _____

   How I feel about meeting this expectation:

   _____

   _____

3. Who: _____

   Expectation: _____

   _____

How I feel about meeting this expectation:

_____

_____

Think it, talk it, Live it, show it.
What ever you want, Let the
universe know it!
—**Michael Dooley**

Do you think it's good that others have expectations for you? Why?

_____

_____

_____

What I Expect of Others

With so many people to please, we can feel as if everyone has more say-so in our lives than we do. Always doing the things they expect of us can make us feel as if we are not true to ourselves (even though this may not be a fact). It helps to realize that expectations are a part of almost all relationships.

Just as others "expect" things of you, you have expectations of them. For example, you expect your parents to buy groceries and to prepare food to eat.

List two people from whom you expect things. What do you expect from each of them? What do you think they think about meeting these expectations?

EXAMPLE:

Who: My friend.

Expectation: I want my boy/girl friend to make plans for us to go somewhere or do something together every weekend.

How I think my friend feels about meeting this expectation: I think he/she almost always wants us to do something together on the weekend, too; although sometimes he might wish he could skip a weekend and just hang out with his friends.

EXAMPLE:

Who: My little sister.

Expectation: When my friends come over to my house after school to do homework or just to hang out, I expect my little sister to understand that I'm entitled to spend some private time with them without her hanging around with us, and that excluding her doesn't mean we don't like her.

How I think my little sister feels about meeting this expectation: I think it's hard for my little sister to understand that I'm entitled to spend time alone with my friends especially when she looks up to me and my friends and loves to be around us older girls.

1. Who: _____

   Expectation: _____

   _____

   How I think _____ feels about meeting this

   expectation _____

   _____

2. Who: _____

Expectation: _____

_____

How I think _____ feels about meeting this

expectation:_____

_____

Do you think it's good that we have
expectations for others? Why?

_____

_____

List someone with whom you find it easy to
compromise and explain why it's easy for you to
meet each person halfway.

Person: _____

Why it's easy to meet this person halfway: ___

_____

_____

_____

Learn from the past, live in the present, plan for the future.
—**Carushka**

Drawing the Line

Sometimes, there's a fine line between going along, doing the things others want you to do, and being true to yourself—listening to your own voice and preferences, acting on what you believe, and doing what's important and best for you.

What does this saying mean to you?

_____

_____

_____

Where do you draw the line between doing what others want and being true to yourself? Write about a time you were "true to your own color"—the self you know better than anyone else does—though you knew that someone special wouldn't think you were cool for making the choice you did. What was the situation? What was going on? Why weren't you and the other person in agreement? How did you stick up for yourself?

_____

_____

_____

How did things turn out? How did what happened affect the relationship between the two of you? Did your friend think you were a "loser" for not going along with him or her, or did that person admire you for sticking with your decision, regardless of how he or she felt about it? How did the way things turned out make you feel?

_____

_____

_____

Self-Worth: What I Think of Me

Self-worth—what we think about ourselves—shows up in the things we say and do. We may even misinterpret the words and actions of others because of the view we hold of ourselves.

What does this saying mean to you?

_____

_____

_____

How does your self-worth show up in the things you say and do? List two ways.

Example: I think of myself as a good student, so I finish my homework every day.

Example: I think of myself as shy, so I don't always talk to people.

1. _____

_____

2. _____

_____

How does the view you hold of yourself show up in the way you feel others think of you?

Example: I think of myself as a poor student, so when the teacher doesn't call on me, I think it's because she sees me as not having the right answer. But in fact, she could think I always have the right answer, so she wants to give some other student a chance.

Example: I think of myself as outgoing, so when someone waves in my direction, I just know they're waving at me—when in fact they could be waving at the person behind me.

❤ _____

_____

_____

the way things turned out?

_____

_____

_____

_____

Write about a time when you saw someone being critical of someone you knew. What was happening? Where did this occur? Who was involved? Why was this person being critical?

_____

_____

_____

How did it make you feel to be around someone who was critical—even though it wasn't you this person was criticizing? How did it influence you? What did you do? Did you say anything to the person who was being critical? Did you say anything to the person being criticized? Why? Then what happened?

_____

_____

_____

_____

How did you feel about yourself for what you did or didn't do? How did this contribute to your sense of self?

_____

_____

_____

_____

Being a Positive Person

Write about a time when you stuck up for someone—even though you didn't know that person all that well. What was going on? What were the circumstances? Where did the incident take place? Who was being critical and why? Why did you stick up for the person being criticized?

_____

_____

_____

How did the person being critical feel about what you did? Were you with friends at the time, or alone? If you were with friends, how did they side with you or remain neutral?

_____

_____

_____

How did you feel about yourself for doing what you did? How did this contribute to your positive sense of self?

_____

_____

_____

How do you think your friends felt about what you did? In what ways were your actions influential—what did they "teach" others?

_____

_____

_____

Decisions: Believing in Myself

I like it when other people encourage me. So it only makes sense that I encourage me, too. It helps me to feel better about myself and then I actually do better.

—Dan Belana, 17

How does feeling better about yourself actually help you do better?

_____

_____

_____

How do you encourage and root for yourself? Write two positive things you can do to encourage yourself.

Example: When I have a bad day, I remind myself of all the things that were positive in my day.

Example: When something doesn't turn out the way I planned (and it's because I've goofed up), I tell myself I'm going to work on doing better, and I trust myself to keep working toward my personal best.

1. _____

   _____

   _____

2. _____

   _____

   _____

Learning ... Growing ... Changing ... Becoming

As we go about our lives, learning and growing, we keep changing or re-creating ourselves, each creation moving closer to who we really are. We already hold a picture of that person in our minds.

Close your eyes and picture yourself in your mind's eye. Who are you? Think of the best "you" that you can imagine and then describe this "you."

WHO I Am ... Who I REALLY Am ... Who I Am

_____

_____

_____

_____

_____

_____

The work of life is to grow closer to who we really are, closer to the image of the person we know ourselves to be deep down.

What does this saying mean to you?

_____

_____

_____

❤ _____

_____

_____

Seeing yourself in the most positive light—believing and trusting in you—can help you do better and to "be" a better person. When things are going good, it's pretty easy to have a positive attitude about yourself. But when the going gets tough, it is also important to believe and trust that you can make it through. Staying positive can be a big help.

Write about a time when things weren't going your way and you decided to look on the bright side. What was going on?

_____

_____

_____

_____

Why weren't things going your way? Who was involved? How did your positive attitude and believing in yourself make a difference in

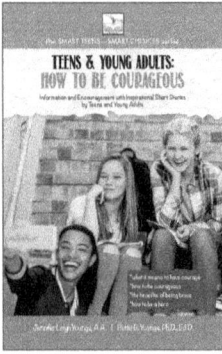

How to Be Courageous

Encouragment and Inspirational Short Stories by Teens and Young Adults
Jennifer Leigh Youngs, A.A. | Bettie B. Youngs, Ph.D., Ed.D.

- *the importance of being courageous*
- *the benefits of being brave*
- *how to be a hero*

Book: 978-1-940784-93-9
e-book: 978-1-940784-92-2

Growing Your Confidence and Self-Esteem

Information, Encouragement and Inspirational Short Stories by Teens and Young Adults
Jennifer Leigh Youngs, A.A. | Bettie B. Youngs, Ph.D., Ed.D.

- *being on good terms with YOU*
- *feeling "good enough"*
- *the power of confience*
- *liking the face in the mirror*
- *being happy and "forward looking"*

Book: 978-1-940784-86-1
e-book: 978-1-940784-87-8

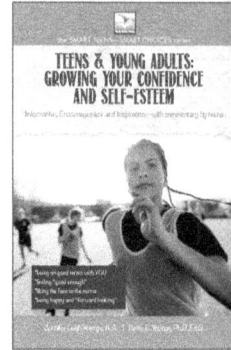

Faith at Work in Our Lives

Information, Encouragement and Inspirational Short Stories by Teens and Young Adults
Jennifer Leigh Youngs, A.A. | Bettie B. Youngs, Ph.D., Ed.D.

- *talking faith with your friends*
- *faith as an anchor in your life*
- *accepting and caring for others*
- *faith in victories and defeats*

Book: 978-1-940784-78-6
e-book: 978-1-940784-79-3

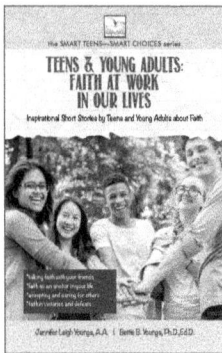

Understanding Feelings of Love

Inspirational Short Stories by Teens and Young Adults
Jennifer Leigh Youngs, A.A. | Bettie B. Youngs, Ph.D., Ed.D.

- *the lessons of love*
- *setting boundaries important to you*
- *4 ways to be a great boy/girlfriend*
- *when love relationships end*

Book: 978-1-940784-75-5
e-book: 978-1-940784-74-8

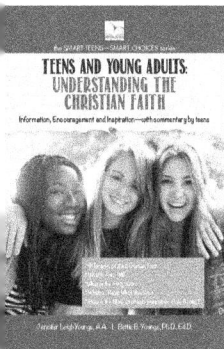

Understanding the Christian Faith

Information, Encouragement and Inspirational Short Stories by Teens and Young Adults

Jennifer Leigh Youngs, A.A. | Bettie B. Youngs, Ph.D., Ed.D.

- *9 Tenants of the Christian Faith*
- *What is Free Will*
- *What is the Holly Spirit*
- *What is "Reap What You Sow"*
- *How is the Bible as unique from other Holy Books?*

Book: 978-1-940784-76-2
e-book: 978-1-940784-77-9

How to be a Good Friend

Information and Encouragement with Inspirational Short Stories
by Teens and Young Adults

Jennifer Leigh Youngs, A.A. | Bettie B. Youngs, Ph.D., Ed.D.

- *understanding friendships*
- *how to be a good friend*
- *making, keeping, and ending friendships*
- *mending hurt feelings*

Book: 978-1-940784-73-1
e-book: 978-1-940784-72-4

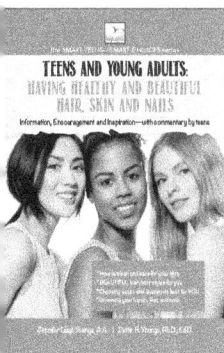

Having Healthy and Beautiful Hair, Skin and Nails

Information, Encouragement and Inspiration—with commentary by teens

Jennifer Leigh Youngs, A.A. | Bettie B. Youngs, Ph.D., Ed.D.

- *how to clean and care for your skin*
- *BEAUTIFUL hair; best styles for you*
- *choosing soaps and shampoos best for YOU*
- *grooming your hands, feet, and nails*

Book: 978-1-940784-84-7
e-book: 978-1-940784-85-4

The Power of Being Kind, Courteous and Thoughtful

Information, Encouragement and Inspirational Short Stories by Teens and Young Adults

Jennifer Leigh Youngs, A.A. | Bettie B. Youngs, Ph.D., Ed.D.

- *the power of being KIND*
- *the importance of being COURTEOUS*
- *how to be "THOUGHTFUL"*

Book: 978-1-940784-82-3
e-book: 978-1-940784-83-0

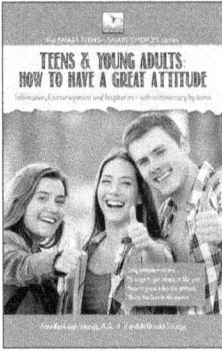

How to Have a Great Attitude
Information, Encouragement and Inspirational Short Stories by Teens and Young Adults
Jennifer Leigh Youngs, A.A. | Bettie B. Youngs, Ph.D., Ed.D

- *food—your body's source of energy*
- *sleep—restores body and brain*
- *liking the face in the mirror*
- *stress, anxiety, and emotional ups and downs*

Book: 978-1-940784-90-8
e-book: 978-1-940784-91-5

Caring for Your Body's Health and Wellness
Information, Encouragement and Inspirational Short Stories by Teens and Young Adults
Jennifer Leigh Youngs, A.A. | Bettie B. Youngs, Ph.D., Ed.D.

- *food—your body's source of energy*
- *sleep—restores body and brain*
- *liking the face in the mirror*
- *stress, anxiety, and emotional ups and downs*

Book: 978-1-940784-88-5
e-book: 978-1-940784-89-2

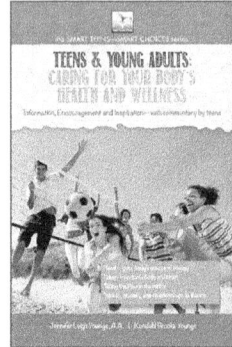

TEEN TOWN PRESS
www.TeenTownPress.com

www.BettieYoungsBooks.com
info@BettieYoungsBooks.com

AVAILABLE ON-LINE
and from the
INGRAM BOOK COMPANY

Bettie Youngs Publishing Co., Inc.
www.BettieYoungsBooks.com
info@BettieYoungs.com

Foreign Rights:
Sylvia Hayse Literary Agency, LLC
hayses@caat.com

www.ingramcontent.com/pod-product-compliance
Lightning Source LLC
Chambersburg PA
CBHW021343090426
42742CB00008B/721